T0026726

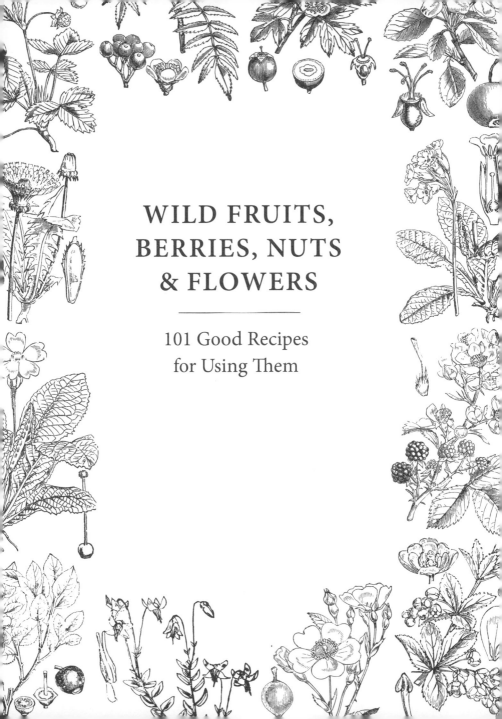

WILD FRUITS, BERRIES, NUTS & FLOWERS

101 Good Recipes for Using Them

Elder-flower

WILD FRUITS, BERRIES, NUTS & FLOWERS

101 Good Recipes for Using Them

by B. JAMES

Foreword by Barbara Segall

PIMPERNEL
PRESS LTD
www.pimpernelpress.com

When foraging for wild food, **you must be able to correctly identify what you are picking**, otherwise you should not eat it. Never eat any wild food without multiple sources of positive identification – do not eat any wild fruits, flowers, or mushrooms just from reading this book.

BARBARA SEGALL grows fruit, veg and herbs, as well as ornamental garden plants in her town garden in the countryside. Her daily walks are the starting point for her hedgerow foraging for elder, nettles, sloes and bullace, which she turns into kitchen produce. She also forages much from her own garden. She writes articles, books and blogs about gardens, grow your own and herbs (www.thegardenpost.com). She edits *The Horticulturist* and is a member of the Garden Media Guild and also of the Guild of Food Writers.

Pimpernel Press Limited
www.pimpernelpress.com

Wild Fruits, Berries, Nuts & Flowers
© Pimpernel Press Limited 2021

All rights reserved. No part of this publication may be reproduced, stored in a retrieval system or transmitted, in any form, or by any means, electronic, mechanical, photocopying, recording or otherwise, without prior permission in writing from the publisher or a licence permitting restricted copying. In the United Kingdom such licences are issued by the Copyright Licensing Agency, Hay's Galleria, Shackleton House, 4 Battle Bridge Lane, London SE1 2HX.

A catalogue record for this book is available from the British Library.

ISBN 978-1-914902-98-7

Typeset in Minion Pro
Printed and bound in China
9 8 7 6 5 4 3 2 1

The publishers have made every effort to contact holders of copyright works. Any copyright holders we have been unable to reach are invited to contact the publishers so that a full acknowledgment may be given in subsequent editions.

MIX
Paper from
responsible sources
FSC® C008047

CONTENTS

Dog Rose

FOREWORD

Harvesting from hedgerows seems to be in my DNA. I have been foraging for flowers, fruit, foliage and mushrooms from hedgerow, field edges – and from my own garden – for decades. Collecting and using wild-grown food is something that earlier generations would have done out of need to supplement a meagre diet. For me it is not a necessity but something I enjoy doing from season to season.

I think it started with the blackthorn – thorny and woody hedgerow trees that I first encountered when I moved from London to the Suffolk countryside. Their small round fruits called sloes, with the most dive-in-deep blue bloom on their skins, are too sharp to eat from the tree. But if you steep them in gin and sugar the result is a perfect transformation into an oh-so-delectable fruit liqueur.

A short while after I started to make annual batches of sloe gin I came across this book, *Wild Fruits, Berries Nuts & Flowers 101 Good Recipes for Using Them* by B. James M.C.A., published by The Medici Society. It was listed in a catalogue I subscribed to from Books for Cooks based in Rottingdean, Sussex. It was made for me – a guide that offered gentle, unfussy and definitely unbossy information on how to use the fruits I found in the wild or at my garden's edge.

Try as I might I have not been able to find out who B. James was and if he or she had written any other books about wild harvesting or foraging, as it is now popularly known. The book was published in 1942 when wartime rationing was still in place. It was a time of shortages when wild-harvesting made a difference to what might be on the plate for a hungry family to eat.

The last note in the book is about substitutes for fresh lemons, which the note says are 'now unobtainable'. It is hard to imagine such shortages today when we can buy a bundle of lemons in every market and supermarket all year round. The note offers additional good-to-know information if you are making wines and beers you could use rhubarb, green apple or gooseberry juice as a substitute for the lemons!

For me the annual sloe foraging sequence starts in spring when I note a few blackthorn trees that are thickly covered with white blossom. Then I wait patiently as the fruits form and swell to a reasonable size before harvesting them on a late summer or early autumn day.

Sometimes, if I am too busy to process them immediately I wash and bag them for the freezer. This also means that I can get past the first step, which, although satisfying, is a little time-consuming. Each sloe has to be pricked in several places with a needle to hasten the maceration of the fruit. As I prick each blue sloe, one-by-one I drop them into a bottle, half filled with gin. Next I add sugar and a good pinch of patience, waiting several months before drinking. The resulting, rich and full-bodied liquor is the one that will get me through the grey, cold evenings in winter. Particularly good for sipping in armchair by the fireside!

I was fortunate that I had bullaces and damsons growing in the field-edge hedge at the boundary of my first country garden in Suffolk. Bullaces are edible but also suit similar alcoholic pairing, but this time my choice is to pair them with vodka. Damsons are my choice for the most kingly purple and sharply tasty tubs of ice cream or sorbets.

So the move from city to countryside was the trigger for me to become a home and hedgerow forager. There is something very

satisfying about harvesting produce that grows freely in the wild
or like the bullaces in my hedgerow, are wild and not planted by
me. Equally satisfying is transforming the harvest produce in your
kitchen into something delicious to use immediately or store for
later use.

There are of course a few ground rules that you need to have in mind
when you begin to forage. First of all your own safety is paramount.
Only harvest from plants that you know are not poisonous and
always avoid any that are too close to roads (fumes as well as safety)
or might have been sprayed or otherwise contaminated in some way.

Next, never dig up wild plants as they are protected and you would
need permission. If what you want to harvest is on private property,
get permission from the owner to go on the property and to pick.

Never over-pick. Only pick what you will use in one session. Leave
some for other foragers, or for wildlife to feast on and also for the
plants to set seed for next year's harvest. Always wash the material
you harvest when you get it home, since it might have been sullied in
some way.

My forage year usually starts in spring when elder flowers are just
opening. I set out on a walk with a cloth bag and a pair of scissors
and use my walking stick to bring any branches that are too far off
to reach, a bit closer to me. I sometimes take a pair of secateurs,
especially if I am picking sloes off their thorny stems. Whatever you
do don't set out with a knife, as that would be completely illegal.

Once you have started foraging you will want to know how to use
the produce you have harvested. This book is divided into sections.
The largest deals with fruits, including rose hips and crab-apples.

Next flowers are covered, followed by nuts. The last section covers seaweed and mosses, neither of which have I ever foraged for. This section does also include truffles and field mushrooms, both of which I have foraged for with great success. I found summer truffles growing at the base of a birch tree in my own garden. This book doesn't cover other mushrooms or fungi that you are more likely to come across such as puff balls, chanterelles and St George's mushroom. But there are many books, courses and websites devoted simply to identification and foraging for mushrooms, as well as for using them.

In terms of what to do with the material you harvest, this book covers making jams, baking, pickling and creating alcoholic drinks. I have always made jams, jellies, chutney, and various alcoholic drinks with my foraged harvests.

For information on other techniques such as fermenting and pasteurizing you may have to use other publications or search online.

Just google foraging courses and you will find a huge range to choose from to guide you. There are many excellent books written by modern foragers including Richard Mabey's seminal *Food for Free*, published in 1972; John Lewis-Stempel's *Foraging* complete with a calendar of monthly harvests; Roger Phillips' *Wild Food, a Complete Guide for Foragers* (first published in 1983), and Liz Knight's bang up-to-date *Forage*.

When I began my intermittent seasonal foraging there was not much guidance and foraging was hardly mainstream. Now there is so much information and there are also many courses that you can take. I feel fortunate that I had this book for my guide and now my hope is that this edition published by Pimpernel Press will charm and guide a new set of foragers.

Barbara Segall, Suffolk

USEFUL WEBSITES

WildfoodUK: www.wildfooduk.com

Joint Nature Conservation Committee: https://jncc.gov.uk

Natural England: https://www.gov.uk/government/organisations/natural-england

Countryside Council for Wales https://naturalresources.wales

NatureScot (previously Scottish Natural Heritage): https://www.nature.scot

Marine Stewardship Council: https://www.msc.org/uk

Woodland Trust: www.woodlandtrust.org.uk

INTRODUCTION

GOOD FOOD FROM THE HEDGEROWS

More than 100 years ago a British housewife wrote in her book of 'receipts' the following lines:

"Why has bounteous Nature given,
With full and generous hands.
Fruits of the heath and hedgrow,
And flowers of the dells and sands.
All free to man for the taking,
That he may eat and live?
So take and use them wisely,
While grateful thanks ye give."

In England up to fifty years ago the delicious wild fruits and flowers of the countryside, as well as the vegetables of the sea, were always used and greatly prized.

In their place to-day factory-made foods, synthetic flavourings, vinegars and essences are bought in tins and bottles.

The old flower vinegars and syrups have gone. Rarely we find in old world farmhouses and cottages the wines and jellies once made from berries and flowers.

It has taken a World War to make us realize just what we have lost of the good things of bygone days.

It is difficult to-day to make tasty dishes without fruit, sauces, jams, and flavourings, yet the wild fruits and flowers of the countryside are left to waste and wither.

The luscious plums and strawberries of pre-war days we so fondly remember have come to us from the tiny wild sloes, bullace, and wild strawberry.

Giant dessert blackberries at two shillings a pound are tasteless compared with the wild brambles from which they sprang. Man, in his effort to get size and outward beauty in fruits and flowers has sadly lost in flavour and fragrance.

We have lost nothing from our table to-day that cannot, with little trouble, be replaced from the countryside if only we will gather its harvest.

Why sigh for orange marmalade and blackcurrant pies when the wild rose hips and elderberries will give us something better? Salads need not be dowdy while primroses, violets and roses are in season. We can capture their fragrance in vinegar and syrup and store it for winter use.

Many of the old-world flower-scented pies, puddings, and tarts are worth reviving, not as novelties, but to take the place of much we lack to-day.

For those who would like to try them this small book of recipes is intended.

B.J.

FRUITS

BILBERRIES, WHORTLEBERRIES & BLAEBERRIES 16

Bilberry Jam 17; Bilberry Conserve 17; Bilberry or Whortleberry Jelly 18;
Bilberry Pie 18; Whortleberry Pudding 18; Bilberry or Blaeberry
Muffins 19; Bilberry Soup 19; Bilberry Compote 20; Bilberry Pancakes 20;
Unripe Bilberry Jelly 21; Bilberry and Cranberry Jam 21

BARBERRIES 22

Barberry Marmalade 23; Barberry Jam 23; Barberry Jelly 23

BRAMBLES 24

Spiced Bramble Jelly 24; Bramble and Chilli Jelly 24; Seedless Blackberry
Chutney 25; Blackberry Curd 25; Bramble Cordial 27; Bramble Wine 27;
Blackberry or Bramble Jam 28; Bramble Jelly 28; Bramble Ketchup 28

THE BULLACE 29

Bullace Chutney 29; Bullace Gin 29; Bullace Marmalade 30;
Bullace Jelly 30

CRAB-APPLES 31

Crab-apple Jelly 31; Crab-apple Marmalade 33;
To preserve Crabs Whole 33; Verjuice 33

CRANBERRIES OR FENBERRIES 34

Cranberry Cheese 34; Cranberry Jam 35; Cranberry Sauce 35;
Cranberry Tart 36; Cranberry Jelly (for Green Salads) 36; Cranberry
Jelly (for storing) 37; Spiced Cranberry Sauce 37; Cranberry Ketchup 38;
Cranberry and Apple Jam 38

ELDERBERRIES 39

Elder Syrup 39; Elder Rob 39; Elderberry and Blackberry Jam 40;
Elderberry and Apple Marmalade 40; Elderberry Chutney 41;
Elderberry Ketchup 41; Elder and Blackberry Soup 42; Elderberry Pie 42;
Elderberry Pudding 43; A Piquant Sauce from Hedgerow Berries 43

SLOES OR BLACKTHORN 45

Sloe Jelly 45; Sloe Gin 46; Sloe and Crab-Apple Jelly 46;
Sloe and Apple Jelly 47; Sloe Wine 47

WILD STRAWBERRIES 49

Wild-Strawberry Bowle 49; Wild-Strawberry Ice 50;
Wild-Strawberry Jam 50

ROSE-HIPS 51

Rose-Hip Wine 51; Rose-Hip Soup 51; Rose-Hip Marmalade 53; Hips
in Syrup 53; Chutney from Wild-Rose Berries 54; Rose-Hip Sauce 54;
Sweet-Brier Hips 55; Sweet-Brier Tart 55

ROWAN OR MOUNTAIN ASH 57

Rowan (Mountain-Ash Berry) Jelly 57; Rowan Jelly with Apples 58;
Rowan Wine 58

HAWS 59

Hawthorn Jelly 59; Haw and Crab-Apple Jelly 59; Hawthorn Brandy 61

Bilberry

BILBERRIES, WHORTLEBERRIES AND BLAEBERRIES

Bilberries are called Blaeberries in the Highlands, Whortleberries in South of England. They lack pectin. A little added acid, either rhubarb or tartaric acid is necessary to make fairly well set jam or jelly.

BILBERRY JAM

3 lbs. bilberries.	½ lb. rhubarb.
3 lbs. sugar.	1 tablespoon water.

Cut rhubarb into small pieces. Put into pan with well washed bilberries and water. Simmer gently till fruit quite tender, and mixture fairly thick. Add sugar. Simmer twenty minutes. Test. Continue cooking till set is obtained. Pot in small very dry jars.

BILBERRY CONSERVE

4 lbs. bilberries.	¼ oz tartaric acid.
3 ½ lbs. sugar.	1 tablespoon water.

Simmer fruit, water, and tartaric acid till skins of fruit quite tender. Add sugar. Simmer about twenty-five minutes till conserve fairly thick.

BILBERRY OR WHORTLEBERRY JELLY

Bilberries for jelly should be under ripe but not green. Place fruit in pan, crush a little, simmer in own juice till soft. Strain through jelly bag or double fine muslin. Return juice to pan. When boiling add to each pint 1 lb. sugar. Stir till dissolved. Boil ten minutes. Test and pot.

Can be used as sweet or with game and meat.

BILBERRY PIE

Line a deep pie plate with thin pastry. Cover with thick layer of bilberries and plenty of soft brown sugar. Cover with pastry. Press edges well together. Bake twenty-five or thirty minutes in brisk oven.

Served with cream or custard this North Country speciality is delicious.

WHORTLEBERRY PUDDING

Speciality of the West Country.

Line pudding basin with thin suet pastry. Fill with whortleberries and brown sugar. Cover pastry. Tie over. Steam or boil two to three hours according to size. Serve hot with cream or custard.

Whortleberry pies are made in deep pie dish. Before cutting, the crust is lifted and cream poured in.

BILBERRY, OR BLAEBERRY MUFFINS

An American speciality.

1 cup bilberries.
2 cups self-raising flour.
4 tablespoons castor sugar.
2 eggs.

4 tablespoons margarine or butter.
1 cup milk.
Pinch of salt.

Stir together three tablespoons sugar and one tablespoon flour from ingredients. Sprinkle with washed and drained bilberries. Work remainder of ingredients to stiff batter. Stir in fruit lightly, together with an extra teaspoon of baking powder. If plain flour is used three teaspoons of baking powder will be necessary. All cakes made with fresh fruit require extra baking powder to make them light. Half fill greased small round tins. Bake moderate oven thirty minutes.

BILBERRY SOUP

1 lb. ripe bilberries.
1 ¼ pints water.

1 oz. cornflour.
Sugar to taste.

Simmer fruit and water fifteen minutes. Sieve. Thicken with cornflour. Sweeten to taste. Serve hot with tiny boiled dumplings.

BILBERRY COMPOTE

1 lb. bilberries.

3 ozs. sugar.

½ teaspoon cornflour.

Piece stick cinnamon.

Well wash bilberries. Drain them. Mix with sugar. Put in saucepan with small piece of cinnamon and simmer five minutes. Stir in cornflour mixed with dessertspoon water. Simmer two minutes to slightly thicken. Serve cold.

BILBERRY PANCAKES

1 pint milk.

2 eggs.

Pinch salt.

Vanilla essence.

Flour.

¼ pint prepared dry bilberries.

Beat egg, milk, salt, vanilla, with enough flour to make smooth pancake batter firm enough to hold fruit. Stir in bilberries.

Fry pancakes in plenty of fat. Serve piled on top of each other with sugar sprinkled between.

UNRIPE BILBERRY JELLY

1 1lb. red bilberries.
3 small sweet dessert apples,
    not green ones.

1½ lbs. sugar.
1 teacup water.
1 dessertspoon vinegar.

Make syrup with sugar, vinegar, water. While boiling, stir in bilberries, and peeled apples very thinly sliced. Simmer all very slowly till slices of apple are quite transparent.

    Bilberries must be at red stage. Ripe ones will not do.

Cream cheese and red bilberry jelly sandwiches are unusual and very tasty.

BILBERRY AND CRANBERRY JAM
As made in the Colonies.

2 lbs. cranberries.
2 lbs. bilberries.
Sugar.

Wash fruit. Put in pan. Crush to start juice using wooden spoon. Simmer to pulp. Beat well with spoon. Add 14 ozs. sugar to each pound of pulp. Boil about twenty minutes after sugar dissolved.

    Acid of cranberries makes jam good setter.

BARBERRIES

The best of all our wild fruits. Barberries are the bright red, very acid berries of thorny yellow flowered shrubs. Quite common in hedges during autumn.

They make a useful substitute for tamarind in curries.

Barberry

BARBERRY MARMALADE

2 lbs. barberries.
2 lbs. sugar.

Stand fruit and sugar in large jar or basin in a pan of boiling water
until sugar has dissolved. Stir well and leave twenty-four hours. Boil
in preserving pan fifteen minutes. Sets well.

BARBERRY JAM

Wash barberries. Remove all stalk. Put in oven jar or casserole with
lid. Bake in a very slow oven until soft. Press through sieve. Weigh.
Add equal weight of sugar. Stir well and boil for fifteen minutes.

BARBERRY JELLY

Wash and pick over barberries. Put in pan with barely enough water
to cover. Crush them a little. Simmer till fruit very soft.
    Strain through double muslin without squeezing the fruit.
Just let it drip for several hours.
    Add 1 lb. sugar to one pint of juice. When dissolved boil for ten
minutes. It should be firm jelly.

BRAMBLES

SPICED BRAMBLE JELLY

1 lb. brambles.

2 cloves.

1 inch of stick cinnamon.

1 lb. sugar.

¼ pint water.

¼ pint best malt vinegar.

½ small bay leaf.

Stew brambles in water with spices till tender. Press through sieve till only seeds remain.

Return pulp to small pan with vinegar and sugar. Heat a little. Stir till sugar dissolved. Boil twenty minutes. Test and pot. Sufficient to make four small pots of spiced jelly for use with meat and fish.

BRAMBLE AND CHILLI JELLY

3 lbs. ripe brambles.

4 small dried red chillies.

1 dessertspoon lemon juice or pinch tartaric acid.

Sugar.

Put brambles, lemon juice, and broken chillies in pan on warm stove. Crush fruit and leave several hours to draw juice. Strain. Put juice in pan with 1 lb. sugar to each pint. Boil twenty-five to thirty minutes. Test. Pot in small hot jars.

A rather hot sweet jelly for meat and game.

SEEDLESS BLACKBERRY CHUTNEY

2 lbs. ripe blackberries.	½ lb. brown sugar.
1 pint malt vinegar.	Pinch Cayenne pepper.
1 lb. finely chopped apples.	1 oz. salt.
6 ozs. chopped sultanas	1 teaspoon chopped garlic or, shallot.
or raisins.	1 teaspoon ground ginger.

Put vinegar and blackberries in pan. Crush fruit. Simmer thirty
minutes. Sieve, pressing out all juice and fruit pulp. Put in pan with
chopped green applies and sultanas, shallot, spice and salt. Bring
to boil. Add sugar. Cook very gently thirty minutes. Stir in two
teaspoons mustard seed. Bottle.

BLACKBERRY CURD

Very useful as spread or for tart filling. Do not make too much.
It does not keep very long.

1 lb. ripe blackberries.	8 ozs. castor sugar.
1 green apple.	1 lemon.
2 eggs.	4 ozs. butter or margarine.

Put blackberries and chopped apple in saucepan. Crush and simmer
till soft. Do not add water. Press through sieve to take out seeds. Put
pulp, sugar, beaten eggs, butter, grated yellow rind and juice of lemon
in double saucepan. Stir till mixture thickens. Pot and seal. Will keep
two months if airtight.

Blackberry

BRAMBLE CORDIAL

4 lbs. ripe brambles.　　　　　1 lb. sugar.
1 pint malt vinegar.　　　　　Cloves, root ginger.

Put fruit in crock. Crush. Pour over boiling vinegar. Stand twenty-four hours. Strain well. Return to pan with 1 lb. sugar.

To each pint of liquid allow eight cloves and 3 ozs. of best root ginger loosely tied in muslin. Boil thirty minutes. Take out spice. Bottle. Ready for use in forty-eight hours.

Delicious in soda water, or as hot winter drink.

BRAMBLE WINE

Allow 1½ lbs. very ripe brambles to each pint of water used. Put fruit in crock, bruise with wooden spoon, pour over boiling water. Cover with cloth. Stand seven days, stirring twice daily. Carefully remove all scum. Strain through fine muslin. Put in pan with 6 ozs. sugar to each pint juice. Gradually heat and stir till sugar melted. Do not allow to boil. Bottle and allow to ferment uncorked.

When fermentation ceases strain into fresh bottles and cork. Improves by keeping.

BLACKBERRY OR BRAMBLE JAM

2 lbs. brambles.	2 tablespoons water.
2 lbs. sugar.	1 small lemon, or 1 level teaspoon tartaric acid.

Fruit must only just be ripe. Put in pan with water and acid. Simmer till fruit quite tender and liquid well reduced. Add sugar. Boil fifteen minutes. If fruit over ripe, or less sugar used, jam will not set or keep well.

BRAMBLE JELLY

2 lbs. brambles.	1 small lemon, or tartaric acid.
2 tablespoons water.	Sugar.

Put berries, water, and acid in pan. Crush fruit well. Simmer till quite tender and pulped. Strain through double muslin or jelly bag. Weigh liquid. Return to pan with 1 lb. sugar to each pound juice. Boil briskly fifteen to twenty minutes till sets when tested.

BRAMBLE KETCHUP

4 lbs. brambles.	1 teaspoon allspice.
2 lbs. soft brown sugar.	1 small blade of mace.
2 cups vinegar.	1 dessertspoon each cloves and cinnamon stick.

Boil fruit, vinegar, and spice tied in muslin for ten minutes. Add sugar. Simmer all one-and-a-half to two hours till fruit tender. Bottle.

THE BULLACE

All our luscious dessert plums have been cultivated from the small wild bullace and the sloe. Hard and round, with dark green purplish skin. Requires more sugar and much more cooking than any other wild fruit.

BULLACE CHUTNEY

2 lbs. bullace.
2 large green apples.
2 large onions.
6 ozs sultanas or raisins.
2 teaspoons salt

1½ pints vinegar.
½ oz. each cloves and root ginger.
1 dried red chilli.
½ oz. dry mustard.
1¼ lbs. sugar

Simmer bullaces in water till tender but not broken. Drain well. Remove stones. Chop coarsely. Put in pan with other ingredients finely chopped. Spices to be tied loosely in muslin. Pour over vinegar. Simmer thirty minutes. Add sugar. Boil till nicely thickened.

BULLACE GIN

1 lb. bullace.
8 ozs. crushed sugar candy, or sugar.

1 bottle gin.

Wipe bullace clean, prick several times with needle. Put into jar or large bottle with sugar. Pour over gin. Make airtight. Can be used in six weeks.

BULLACE MARMALADE

Bullace.
Sugar.
Water.

Wash bullace. Put in pan with just enough water to cover. Simmer till tender. Strain but save liquid. Stone bullace. Chop coarsely. Put fruit in pan with one gill of liquid in which boiled, and 1 lb. sugar to each pound of stoned fruit. When sugar dissolved boil briskly fifteen minutes. Should set well when tested.

BULLACE JELLY

For meat dishes.

Take 1 lb. bullace. Simmer till quite tender. Drain. Stone and press through sieve. Add to pulp 6 ozs. sugar, pinch salt and Cayenne pepper to taste. Simmer till thickens. Pot and seal.

Keeps three months. If required to keep longer more sugar must be used.

CRAB-APPLES

Scrab, or crab apples often grow wild in fields and hedgerows. Well armed with thorns, very small and brightly red when ripe, they make delicious jelly and jam.

They are far too tart to be eaten in raw state.

CRAB-APPLE JELLY

1 lb. crab apples.
1 pint water.

Wash crabs, cut in half without peeling or coreing them. Put in pan with water. Simmer gently till tender. Strain through jelly bag or double muslin. Measure liquid. To each pint allow 1 lb. sugar, three cloves. Two teaspoons lemon juice. Put in pan. Very slowly bring to boil, stirring till sugar dissolved. Boil briskly ten to twelve minutes. Jelly should set well when tested. When ready, pot. Cover immediately.

Crab-apple

CRAB-APPLE MARMALADE

A rather tart thick preserve useful for breakfast table. Peel and core largest ripe crabs. Cut thin slices. Put in pan with just a little water. Simmer till pulped. Stir frequently. When soft press through sieve. Weigh pulp and add equal weight of sugar. Stir till dissolved.

Boil gently ten minutes. Stir and watch whole time. It burns easily.

TO PRESERVE CRABS WHOLE

Wash small perfect apples. Dry them. Prick all over with needle to prevent skins bursting. Leave stalks on.

Make a syrup of 1 lb. sugar to half pint of water according to quantity of apples used. When clear add apples, a little red colouring, lemon juice, and one piece of root ginger. The fruit must be covered with syrup. Simmer slowly and gently till apples tender but unbroken. Remove ginger. Bottle in syrup and seal well.

VERJUICE

Verjuice, so often mentioned in high class recipes, is juice pressed out of raw crab-apples and fermented. It is more tart than lemon juice.

CRANBERRIES or FENBERRIES

Cranberries grow abundantly in England on heaths and in mountain districts. The bright red sub-acid berries make many delicious things.

CRANBERRY CHEESE

A good jelly for serving with cold game and white meat. Wash cranberries in running water. Weigh. Put in pan with half a pint of water to each pound of fruit. Simmer gently till soft. Sieve or beat to pulp with wooden spoon.

Add ½ lb. sugar to each pound of pulp. Bring slowly to boil, stirring all the time. Cook eight minutes. Pot and seal.

Cranberry

CRANBERRY JAM

3 lbs. cranberries.
3 lbs. white sugar.
½ pint water.

Wash cranberries. Simmer in the water gently till quite tender,
stirring frequently. Add sugar. When quite dissolved boil jam briskly
for twelve minutes. Should set well when tested.

CRANBERRY SAUCE

For poultry.

1 lb. washed cranberries.
1 pint water.

Simmer together twenty minutes. Crush to pulp with wooden spoon.
Add 6 to 8 ozs. sugar. Simmer fifteen minutes. Pot and stand twenty-
four hours before using. The sauce can be made sweeter through 8
ozs. is usually sufficient.

CRANBERRY TART

1½ pints washed cranberries.   1 oz. butter.
1 cup sugar.   ¾ pint water.

Simmer berries and water till tender. Pulp. Add butter and sugar. Cook one minute after sugar quite dissolved.

Line pie dish with thin pastry. Pour in mixture when cold. Decorate top with thin strips of twisted pastry. Bake in moderate oven till pastry golden brown.

CRANBERRY JELLY

For Green Salads.

Wash cranberries. Put in pan with a little water. Simmer till tender. Pulp and sweeten to taste. Stir in sufficient softened gelatine to set to firm jelly.

When cold cut out strips or fancy shapes to garnish top of green salads.

CRANBERRY JELLY

For storing.

Wash berries. Put in pan with half a pint of water to each pound fruit. Boil gently thirty minutes. Skim well. Strain through muslin. To each pint of juice and 1 lb. white sugar. Boil about twenty minutes. When sets pot and tie over.

If colour too pale a few drops of colouring matter may be added.

SPICED CRANBERRY SAUCE

2 pints washed berries.
½ pint water.
2 teacups brown sugar.
2 teaspoons lemon juice or good vinegar.

1 teaspoon mixed spices.
6 extra cloves.
12 extra pimentoes (allspice)

Put fruit, water, and spices loosely tied in muslin in pan. Simmer till soft. Remove spice. Rub pulp through sieve or beat to very smooth paste. Stir in sugar. When dissolved simmer two minutes.

When cool, pot.

CRANBERRY KETCHUP

3 lbs. cranberries.
1½ lbs. sugar.
¾ pint best malt vinegar.
1 dessertspoon each allspice, cinnamon.

¼ oz. cloves, 3 dried red chilles.
1 teaspoon salt.
Pinch pepper.

Tie spices loosely in muslin. Put in pan with fruit and half the vinegar. Simmer ten minutes. Add all other ingredients. Simmer very gently one hour. Remove spicebag when sufficiently seasoned. Beat well till fruit pulped. When cool put in wide-necked bottles.

CRANBERRY AND APPLE JAM

2 lbs. green apples.
2 lbs. cranberries.

3 gills water.
4½ lbs. sugar.

Put chopped apples and cranberries in pan with water. Simmer gently till tender. Add sugar. Stir till dissolved. Boil ten minutes. Stir frequently, it burns really easily. Test. When sets pot and seal well.

ELDERBERRIES

Elder trees grow abundantly in all parts of the country. Flowers, fruit and buds can be used.

ELDER SYRUP

Put several quarts of clean ripe elderberries into large jar. All stalks must be removed. Place in slow oven or large pan of boiling water to extract juice. Crush well with wooden spoon. Strain syrup through muslin and squeeze out all juice from berries. To each pint of juice add ½ lb. sugar and six cloves. Bring to boil. Simmer very gently five minutes. When quite cold, strain and bottle. Bottles should be small and very well sealed.

In a large bottle opened frequently the syrup may not keep well.

ELDER ROB

Extract juice from fruit as for syrup. To each point of juice add 1 lb. Demerara sugar, a small piece of root ginger and three or four cloves. Spice must be loosely tied in muslin. Boil gently thirty minutes. Remove spice bag as soon as syrup is sufficiently spiced. It must not remain the thirty minutes. Strain through muslin. Bottle when cold.

Both Elder Rob and syrup are excellent for colds. One tablespoonful in small glass of hot water.

ELDERBERRY AND BLACKBERRY JAM

Elderberries alone will not make a firm jam. Mixed with ripe
blackberries they make a preserve equal to the best blackcurrant.
Take equal quantities of elders and blackberries. Put into pan, crush
to start juice, boil gently twenty minutes. No water must be added.
Add 12 ozs. sugar to each pound of pulp. Boil twenty minutes.

ELDERBERRY AND APPLE MARMALADE

A useful recipe to use windfall apples.

6 lbs. apples, peeled, cored and sliced.
1 pint strained elderberry juice.

Put in pan, simmer together till tender. Add 1 lb. sugar to each pound
pulp, grated yellow rind and strained juice of one lemon. Boil gently
till mixture thickens. Pot and cover immediately. The marmalade
can be made without lemon. It will just be a little sweeter. Has good
pink colour.

ELDERBERRY CHUTNEY

2 lbs. ripe elderberries.	1 teaspoon salt.
1 medium chopped onion.	1 teaspoon allspice.
1 chopped green apple.	1 teaspoon mustard seed.
1 pint malt vinegar.	2 small dried chillies.
4 ozs. Demerara sugar.	

Remove berries from green stalks. Mash to pulp. Put in pan with finely chopped apple and onion, spice loosely tied in muslin and vinegar. Simmer twenty minutes. Add sugar and salt. Boil together stirring frequently, till mixture thickens. Pour into dry jars. Tie over at once.

ELDERBERRY KETCHUP

Take one pint ripe elderberries. Put in jar with one pint of boiling good malt vinegar. Stand in warm place twenty-four hours. Strain off without pressing fruit. Place in pan with one very finely chopped shallot, a blade of mace, small piece of root ginger, one teaspoon cloves and one teaspoon peppercorns. Boil for six minutes.

When quite cold bottle with spices left in. An excellent ketchup for fish dishes.

ELDER AND BLACKBERRY SOUP

½ lb. ripe elderberries.
½ lb. blackberries.
1 oz. cornflour.

1½ pints water.
Sugar.

Simmer fruit in water till soft. Sieve. Thicken cornflour. Sweeten.
Serve very hot with small dumplings or hot boiled rice.

ELDERBERRY PIE

Very ripe black elderberries.
Brown sugar, or golden syrup.
Warm water.

Good piecrust.
2 or 3 cloves.

Nearly fill deep pie dish with large black elderberries. They must be
fully ripe. Well sweeten with Demerara sugar or golden syrup. Pour
over two or more tablespoons hot water according to size of pie.
Cover with good rich piecrust. Bake brisk oven till crust browned.
Lower heat and allow fruit to simmer further ten to fifteen minutes.
   Quite equal to blackcurrant pie.

ELDERBERRY PUDDING

Same ingredients as for pie. Spiced fruit mixture is boiled or steamed in suet pastry two-and-a-half to three hours.

A PIQANT SAUCE FROM HEDGEROW BERRIES

A favourite sauce of the Northern countryside where berries are plentiful. Used with roast meats and poultry.

1 pint each elderberries, haws, and rowanberries.
1 quart brown vinegar.
1 lb. soft brown sugar.
1 lb. minced onions.
4 ozs. coarse cooking salt (not table salt).
Spicebag containing 1½ ozs. peppercorns, 20 cloves, a blade of mace and ¼ oz all-spice (pimentoes).

Put all ingredients into pan. Simmer gently for three hours. Remove spice bag and rub mixture through fine sieve to keep back tiny stones. Bottle sauce when quite cold.

Blackthorn

SLOES OR BLACKTHORN

Small almost black berries, somewhat like small damsons of bitter dry flavour. Make delicious jam and wine.

SLOE JELLY

Sloes.
Sugar.
Water.

Wash sloes well and prick all over with needle. Put into pan with just enough water to cover. Bring to boil and simmer gently for two hours. Strain through jelly bag or double muslin. Do not squeeze fruit. Weigh liquid. Add equal weight of sugar. Boil briskly ten to fifteen minutes.

Very good jelly for game and meat.

SLOE GIN

Select ripe perfect sloes. Prick each one in several places with large needle. Half fill wide-necked large bottles or Kilner jars. Shake into each one 2 ozs. crushed sugar candy, or loaf sugar. Fill up with unsweetened gin. Cork or fasten down tightly. Store in warm place two or three months. Shake each bottle once a week. Strain and bottle. Improves with keeping.

Do not throw away the sloes after making the gin. They will keep in airtight jar. One or two in a fruit salad or apple pie improve the flavour.

SLOE AND CRAB-APPLE JELLY

Take equal weight of sloes and crabs. Wash well. Cut crabs into quarters without peeling them. Put in pan. Just cover with water. Boil to pulp, crushing fruit with wooden spoon. Strain through bag or double muslin. Allow 1 lb. sugar to each pint juice. Stir till dissolved. Boil rapidly ten minutes. Test. When sets pour small glasses that can be used on table.

SLOE AND APPLE JELLY

1½ lbs. green apples.	Sugar.
2 lbs. ripe sloes.	Water.

Wash apples, chop coarsely without peeling. Wash sloes and remove stalks. Put in pan, add just enough water to cover, boil to pulp. Strain through muslin. Do not squeeze fruit.

Measure liquid. Put in pan with 1 lb. sugar to pint juice. Boil fifteen minutes. Pot.

SLOE WINE

1 quart sloes.	2 lbs. sugar.
1 quart water.	½ small lemon.

Sloes must be perfectly clean and ripe. Prick each one with needle. Put in crock. Pour over boiling water. When nearly cold, crush well with wooden spoon or hands. Stand three days. Strain on to sugar and thinly sliced lemon. Stir occasionally till sugar melted. Pour all into very small spirit or wine barrel. Leave loosely corked few days then fasten down tightly.

Many country people use large stone jars for winemaking in small quantities with very good results.

After twelve months sloe wine is almost as good as port.

Wild Strawberry

WILD STRAWBERRIES

All the luscious strawberries we cultivate to-day have been produced from the tiny wood strawberry, one of our choicest wild fruits.

It is found in woods and thickets, sometimes on banks near ditches, between June and September.

You cannot mistake it. The flavour of the wild strawberry is infinitely better than that of the cultivated fruit. Once you have tasted it you will search for more.

WILD-STRAWBERRY BOWLE

4 ozs. wild strawberries.
2 ozs. castor sugar.
1 bottle Rhine wine.

Sprinkle strawberries with sugar. Pour over half a pint of wine. Cover and leave thirty minutes. Add remainder of wine. Serve icy cold in high glasses with a dash of seltzer water.

Every one who has visited the mountain districts of Switzerland know this drink. We cannot get Rhine wine to-day. Sweet barrel cider used in place of wine makes a refreshing fruit cup.

WILD-STRAWBERRY ICE

1½ lbs. wild strawberries.
½ pint water.
6 ozs. castor sugar.

2 egg whites.
1 tablespoon lemon juice.

Rub berries through fine sieve. Boil water and sugar to thin syrup.
When quite cold stir in fruit, lemon juice, and stiffly whipped egg
whites. Freeze.

WILD-STRAWBERRY JAM

1 lb. wild strawberries.
¾ lb. preserving sugar, not granulated.

Spread fruit on large dish. Sprinkle with half the sugar well crushed
with rolling pin. Stand overnight.

Pour juice from fruit into small pan. Add rest of sugar. Bring
very slowly to boil, stirring all the time. Boil two minutes. Add fruit.
Simmer about twenty minutes. Test. As soon as sets pot in tiny jars.

Wild strawberry jam is never thick. No amount of boiling will
make it really set. The less you boil the better the flavour.

ROSE-HIPS

ROSE-HIP WINE

An old cottager's receipt. 1850.

Wild rose hips.
Sugar.
Water.

Select firm ripe hips. Cut off all stem and tops. Put into crock or large jar that can be made airtight. To each pound of hips allow 1 lb. white sugar, one and a quarter pints of water. Pour boiling water over sugar. When quite dissolved pour lukewarm over hips. Cover with cloth. Stand warm kitchen fourteen days, stirring twice daily. Make quite airtight with three layers of greaseproof paper brushed with flour and water paste. Stand cool dark place six months. Strain off wine carefully through fine muslin. Bottle and cork. Hip wine is equal to good white wine. It becomes quite potent with keeping.

ROSE-HIP SOUP

8 ozs. rose hips.
1½ pints water.
1 oz. cornflour.

Sugar to taste.
Pinch cinnamon.

Wash and prepare hips. Simmer in water till soft. Sieve. Thicken with cornflour. Sweeten. Serve with small dumplings or boiled rice.

Field Rose

ROSE-HIP MARMALADE

2 lbs. ripe hips (seedless).
1 pint water.
Sugar.

Hips must be weighed after seed removed. Put in pan with water.
Simmer till tender. Rub through sieve. Add 1 lb. sugar to each pound
of pulp. Stir till sugar dissolved. Boil till sets when tested. Pot and tie
over at once.

HIPS IN SYRUP

Select the largest hips. Simmer in water gently till tender but
unbroken. Trim of stalks and blossom ends. Remove seeds. To each
pound of fruit take 1 lb. sugar, one dessertspoon water, small pinch
of cinnamon. Dissolve sugar and water. Put in hips and cinnamon.
Simmer till thickens. Pot in small glasses. Tie over immediately.

CHUTNEY FROM WILD-ROSE BERRIES

2 pints wild-rose hips.
1 lb. cooked sieved green-apple pulp.
8 ozs. Demerara sugar.
8 ozs. finely chopped raisins or sultanas.
1 oz. ground ginger.

½ oz. chopped garlic,
   or 1 oz. onion.
½ oz. Cayenne pepper.
1½ ozs. salt, or more if liked.
1 pint white vinegar.

Wash berries and take out seeds. Chop them and put with raisins to soak in the vinegar for three or four hours.

Put in pan with all other ingredients. Bring to boil and simmer till mixture thickens. Pot and cover at once.

ROSE-HIP SAUCE

Remove seeds from one pint Rose Hips. Simmer in a little water till tender. Press through sieve. Add two tablespoons sugar and wineglass of light wine or good cider. Reheat before serving. For use with puddings, blanc-mange, etc.

SWEET-BRIER HIPS

Sweet-brier Hip Sauce was considered a great delicacy in Queen Victoria's day. It was always served at Balmoral.

The hips must be freshly picked. Wash well and drain quite dry. Take out seeds. Simmer fruit in a little rosewater till soft enough to sieve. Sweeten and add a few drops of lemon juice.

SWEET-BRIER TART

A receipt dated 1684.

Wash hips, take out seeds. Boil to pulp with a little water. Rub through sieve. Add fine sugar, cinnamon, ginger and a little lemon juice to taste.

Make into covered tart with very thin pastry. When baked thickly dust top with fine sugar.

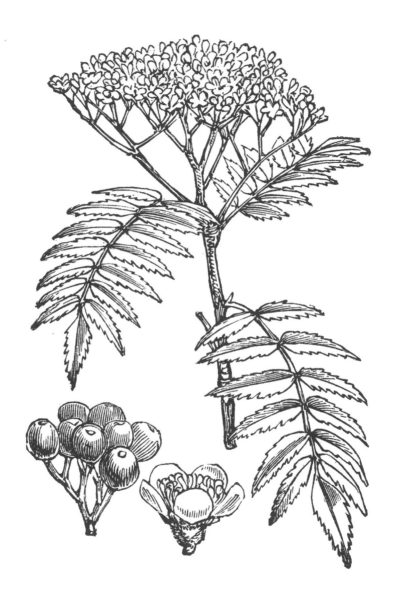

Rowan

ROWAN or MOUNTAIN-ASH

ROWAN (MOUNTAIN-ASH BERRY) JELLY

Rowan berries for jelly must be perfectly ripe and red before skins begin to shrivel.

4 lbs. berries.
1 pint water.

Simmer together and crush well with wooden spoon to get out juice and flavour.

When quite soft and broken strain through jelly bag or double fine muslin. Allow to drip but do not press or squeeze. This will make jelly thick and cloudy.

Weigh 1 lb. sugar to each pint juice. Boil together about one hour till jelly sets when tested.

Hips-and-Haws Jelly can be made on same recipe.

ROWAN JELLY WITH APPLES

Equal quantity of rowans and apples, unpeeled and cut into thick slices. Add just enough water to cover. Simmer till quite soft. Strain through jelly bag or muslin.

To each pint juice add 1 lb. sugar. Boil gently thirty minutes. Test and pot as soon as sets.

Rowan jelly is excellent with meats, game, venison, either hot or cold.

ROWAN WINE

Gather rowans on dry day when quite ripe but not old.

Put in crock, mash them well. Pour over just enough boiling water to cover. Cover with cloth. Stand three days. Drain off liquid without disturbing scum formed on top.

Measure liquid. Put in pan with 1 lb. loaf sugar to each gallon of rowan liquid. Stir till quite dissolved.

Pour into small cask or several large brown stone gallon jars. Cask or jars must be kept quite full while wine working. Leave to work seven days. When working ceases, fasten down tightly. Leave six months. Bottle.

Whenever small quantities of wine of any kind are made brown, stone jars should be used. Very small barrels are difficult to obtain.

HAWS

HAWTHORN JELLY

Wash ripe red haws. Pick them over well. Put in pain with just
enough water to cover. Crush a little. Simmer till quite tender. Strain
though jelly bag or double muslin.

To each pint juice add 1 lb. sugar. Boil gently twenty-five to thirty
minutes. Test. Pot and cover when cold.

HAW AND CRAB-APPLE JELLY

Take equal weight of haws and crab-apples. Small green apples can
also be used. Wash fruit well. Cut apples in quarters without peeling.
If green apples are used cut them coarsely. To each 4 lbs. fruit allow
one pint water, half a teaspoon each ground ginger and cloves.
Simmer till fruit soft. Strain. Add 1 lb. white sugar to each pint juice.
When sugar dissolved boil rapidly about fifteen minutes, when jelly
should set. Test and pot.

Hawthorn

HAWTHORN BRANDY

Select clean white hawthorn petals. No leaves, stalks or centres. Loosely fill bottle with petals. Do not press down. Fill up with brandy. Cork and stand three months. Strain and rebottle.

A potent liqueur. Very fragrant with soda water, or for flavouring. Flowers, when brandy strained off, can be used in trifles.

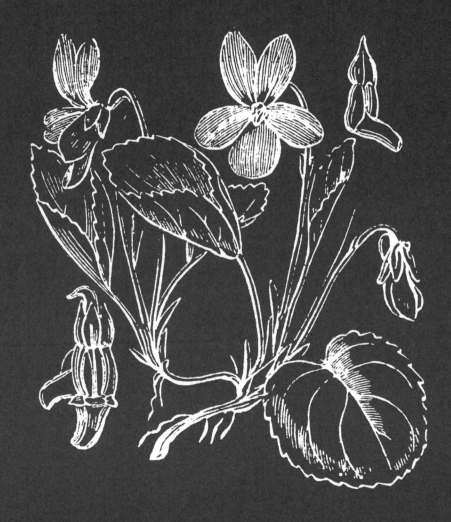

Sweet Violet

FLOWERS

COWSLIPS 65
Cowslip Tart 65; Pickled Cowslips 66; Cowslip Wine 66;
Cowslip Syrup 67; Cowslip Vinegar 67; Cowslip Tea 67

DANDELION 69
Dandelion Puree 69; Dandelion Tea 69; Dandelion Wine 70;
Dandelion Salad 70; Dandelion Beer 71

ELDER-FLOWER 73
Elder-flower Vinegar 73; Elder-flower Pickle 73

PRIMROSE 74
Primrose Tart 74; Primrose Pudding 75; Primrose Vinegar 75

ROSE-PETALS 77
Red-Rose-Petal Jam 77; Rose-petal and Cherry Tart 77;
Rose-Petal and Cherry Salad 78; Rosewater 78

JASMIN 79
Jasmin Scented Tea 79

WILD FLOWERS 80
Wild Flowers for Salads 80; To Save Flowers for Winter Use 80;
Wild Flower Vinegars 81; To Crystallize Flowers 81

Cowslip

COWSLIPS

COWSLIP TART

A favourite sweet of Queen Anne.

1 pint of clean cowslip flowers.

1 egg.

1 small macaroon finely crumbled.

¼ pint cream.

Tiny pinch of salt.

Sugar to taste.

Few drops rosewater.

Mince flowers very finely or pound in a mortar.

Heat cream a little and pour over beaten egg. Stir in all other ingredients. Bake in tiny thin pastry cases, or as a custard pudding in a well buttered dish.

This recipe is delicious made with slightly thickened milk if cream not available.

Fragrance of flowers and rosewater is not lost in cooking.

PICKLED COWSLIPS

1 lb. clean cowslip flowers.
1 lb. sugar.
1 pint white vinegar.

Sprinkle flowers loosely in jar. Boil sugar and vinegar to syrup. Pour at once over flowers and cover.

COWSLIP WINE

1 gallon water.
2 quarts dry cowslip flowers.
3 lbs. sugar.
2 sliced Seville oranges.

2 sliced small lemons.
1 oz. yeast on toast.
Raisins.

Cowslips must be quite fresh and dry. Damp flowers will spoil wine. Put flowers in large crock. Pour boiling water over them. Cover with cloth. Stand three days, stirring several times daily. Strain. Add sugar and boil gently thirty minutes. When nearly cold add yeast. Leave twenty-four hours, or a little longer if necessary, to ferment. Strain liquor into cask. Add half teacup of good raisins to each gallon, and thinly sliced oranges and lemons. No pips must get in. Fasten down well.

Stand ten weeks before bottling.

COWSLIP SYRUP

Take 12 ozs. yellow cowslip flowers. All green must be removed.
Cover with one pint of boiling water. Stand twenty-four hours. Add
2 lbs. best white sugar. Simmer gently to syrup. Strain and bottle.

COWSLIP VINEGAR

1 pint fresh dry cowslip flowers.
1½ pints white wine vinegar.

Place flowers and vinegar in large bottle or jar. Make quite air-tight.
Stand ten to twelve days. Strain and rebottle.

COWSLIP TEA

A countryside remedy for rheumatism. Drink a cup of cowslip tea
four times a week. In several weeks rheumatism is no more.

Allow three teaspoons of flowers to each cup. Put into warmed
teapot. Pour over boiling water. Cover to keep warm. Stand twenty
minutes. Serve with milk, sugar or honey.

Dandelion

DANDELION

DANDELION PUREE

Pick over leaves and wash in several waters. Stand in cold water one hour. Boil in plenty of salted water twenty-five minutes. Turn into colander. Run cold water through them. Squeeze out all water with hands. Chop very finely.

Put in pan 1 oz. butter or margarine, one dessertspoon flour, pepper, salt, and one tablespoon rich gravy. Stir till blended. Add dandelion. Stir with wooden spoon seven or eight minutes till thoroughly hot. Add one tablespoon cream or evaporated milk. Turn into hot dish, garnish with tiny fingers of thin crisp toast.

DANDELION TEA

Scald a handful of yellow dandelion petals in half pint of water. Leave till lukewarm before drinking. A fine spring medicine.

DANDELION WINE

3 quarts dandelion flower heads.	1 large lemon.
1 gallon water.	1 oz. yeast spread on thin toast.
3 lbs. moist sugar.	1 lb. large fleshy raisins.
2 sweet oranges.	

Flowers must be freshly gathered with no stalks at all.

Put into earthen crock or basin. Boil water and pour over them. Cover and leave three days. Stir each day.

Add sugar and yellow rind of oranges and lemon. Keep out the white pith. Boil all one hour. Pour into crock and add pulp of oranges and lemon. When cool put in yeast, cover with a cloth and stand three days. Strain and bottle.

The raisins should be divided between the bottles before wine poured in. Cork very loosely. When fermentation ceases press corks down tightly.

Use after six months. It is very good.

DANDELION SALAD

Select young perfect dandelion leaves. Soak twenty-four hours. Drain and dry. Put in salad bowl with a few chopped chives or young onion tops. Stir in French dressing of oil, vinegar, pepper and salt. Decorate top with yellow dandelion petals.

DANDELION BEER

1 lb. dandelion roots and leaves.	2 lemons.
4 ozs. dandelion petals.	2 lbs. Demerara sugar.
2 ozs. well bruised ginger.	1 oz. yeast spread on toast.
2 gallons water.	2 ozs. cream of tartar.

The dandelion must be well washed and dried before using, and must be freshly gathered.

Put into pan with water and ginger. Boil ten minutes. Pour over sugar, tartar, and sliced lemons. Use an earthenware crock or very large basin.

When nearly cold, put in yeast. Leave for twelve hours.

Strain carefully. Bottle after three days. Will be ready for use in seven days.

Elder-flower

ELDER-FLOWER

ELDER-FLOWER VINEGAR

Put 1 oz. fresh elder flowers in one pint white wine vinegar. Cork well. Stand fourteen days, in sun if possible. Strain and bottle.

ELDER-FLOWER PICKLE

Gather elder flowers just as they begin to open. Fully open flowers soon lose pollen and flavour. They must be quite dry. Pack them in jars. Cover with boiling white wine vinegar. Cover well. Leave fourteen days before using.

Very nice with tender cold meat.

PRIMROSE

PRIMROSE TART

Line a buttered tart tin with thin pastry. Cover with generous layer of sliced apples and castor sugar. Sprinkle well with yellow primrose petals and then with more castor sugar. Cover with pastry and bake in usual way.

Primrose

PRIMROSE PUDDING

An old-world pudding well worth trying.

2 large cups of primrose petals. 3 eggs.
½ lb. fine white bread crumbs. 1 oz. castor sugar, more if liked.
4 ozs. grated suet. 1 third pint of milk.

Well butter mould or basin. Dust inside with castor sugar. Mix crumbs, sugar, and warmed milk. Stir in suet and flowers. Beat in eggs one at a time. Pour mixture into basin, cover buttered paper, steam one-and-a-quarter hours.

Serve with sweet white cornflour sauce flavoured with a glass of Sherry or Marsala.

PRIMROSE VINEGAR

Put one pint of primrose petals in large screwtop jar. Cover with one and a half pints white wine vinegar. Make quite airtight and infuse for fourteen days. Strain and bottle.

Sweet-brier Rose

ROSE-PETALS

RED-ROSE-PETAL JAM

Though not a wild flower many people have roses in profusion. The deep red scented petals should not be wasted, they make the best conserve. The deep pink petals of wild roses can also be used, though colour of jam is not so rosy.

Boil 1 lb. of preserving sugar with one tablespoonful of water to syrup. It must be done slowly.

Wash and dry 1 lb. of rose petals. Stir them in with one dessertspoon of orange flower or rosewater. Both can be purchased in small quantities from chemist if you have none made at home. When well mixed simmer till thickens. Pot in usual way.

Rose petal jam never sets. It is really a thick conserve.

A small quantity on a trifle or milk sweet is delicious.

ROSE-PETAL AND CHERRY TART

Stone sweet red or black cherries. Place in deep pie dish. Sprinkle with sugar and a little water. Cover with generous handful of scented red rose petals. Cover pastry. Bake in usual way. Rose-leaves add delicious scent to fruit.

ROSE-PETAL AND CHERRY SALAD

Sweet cherries.
Cream cheese.
Crisp lettuce leaves.
Scented rose-petals.
Tomato.
Salad cream, or spiced vinegar.

Arrange small dry lettuce leaves in bowl. Stone cherries and press
in a little soft cream cheese. Skin and thinly slice ripe tomatoes.
Arrange tomato and cherries in centre. Garnish round with rose
petals. Top with salad cream. Vinegar must be used sparingly with
this salad, and no salt.

ROSEWATER

For toilet purposes.

Many of the old recipes for making Rosewater are far too elaborate
for the present day.

Take as many scented petals as possible. There must be some red
ones among them to add a pale pink colour to the water.

Cover with rain water and bring slowly to boil. When cold strain.
Will keep fresh and fragrant for several days.

JASMIN

JASMIN SCENTED TEA

The real jasmin scented tea of China is difficult to obtain.

8 ozs. Oolong or green China tea.
1 handful dried Jasmin flowers

Be sure the flowers are from the old fashioned white scented jasmin.
The other varieties may not be eaten.

Make tea in usual way. Sugar may be taken with it but never milk.

Jasmin

WILD FLOWERS

WILD FLOWERS FOR SALADS

Wild-rose and sweet-brier petals. Cowslips. Primroses. Elder-flowers.
White jasmin. Wild violets.

TO SAVE FLOWERS FOR WINTER USE

Dry fresh petals of all salad flowers. Remove all green stalk and petal
tips. Put alternate layers of flowers and sugar till jar full but not too
tightly packed. Fill with best white vinegar. Malt vinegar will not do.
Cork tightly. Keep in cool dry place.

WILD FLOWER VINEGARS

All the salad flowers and red burnet and red-clover petals make sweetly scented vinegars. Prepare petals. Pack loosely in wide-necked bottles. Cover with white wine or good malt vinegar. Seal. Allow to steep ten to fifteen days. Strain into fresh bottles. Cork well.

TO CRYSTALLIZE FLOWERS

Flowers must be quite fresh and all green stalk and leaves removed. Take fine white sugar, add a very little water.

Boil till commences to candy, stirring all the time. Drop flowers into boiling sugar. Not too many, or sugar will not entirely cover petals. Remove from fire. Stir frequently till cold when loose sugar can be sifted from them.

Store in airtight tins in very dry place.

Violets and rose petals for cakes. Mint and peppermint leaves for peppermint creams and chocolates are well worth candying. They are expensive to buy in the shops. Candied peppermint leaves almost unobtainable to-day.

NUTS

HAZEL & FILBERT NUTS 83
Salted or Sugared Hedge Nuts 83; Hazel-Nut Savoury 83;
Nutty Potatoes 85; Burnt Hazel-Nut Toffee 85

HAZEL & FILBERT NUTS

Hazels and Filberts are plentiful in hedges in early autumn. Containing little oil they are easily digested. Shelled, blanched, and minced or grated they can be used on fruit salads, in cakes, puddings, savouries, etc.

SALTED OR SUGARED HEDGE NUTS

Shell. Blanch in hot water one minute and rub on cloth to remove brown skins. Put small amount of butter in thick pan. Fry nuts a pale brown. Drain on paper. Roll in salt or fine sugar while still hot. When quite cold put in airtight bottles.

Quite as nice as salted almonds.

HAZEL-NUT SAVOURY

4 heaped tablespoons grated hazels.	1 small finely chopped onion.
4 large mashed potatoes.	½ pint milk or gravy.
2 ozs. margarine.	Pepper, salt.
1 egg.	Grated cheese.

Mix mashed potatoes, butter, milk, beaten egg in saucepan till smooth. Add nuts, onion, and seasoning. Put into buttered oven dish. Sprinkle top with cheese. Bake moderate oven twenty minutes till nicely browned.

Hazel-nut

NUTTY POTATOES

4 potatoes, baked in skins.   Pinch mixed herbs.
4 tablespoons finely chopped hedge huts.   Pepper, salt.
1 oz. margarine.

Blanch nuts, chop or grate them. Put in pan with butter, gently cook
till lightly browned.

Cut baked potatoes in half. Carefully take out centres. Mash. Add
nuts, herbs and seasoning. Refill halved potato skins. Pile up mixture
in centre. Pour over fat from pan. Reheat and brown in oven and
under griller.

BURNT HAZEL-NUT TOFFEE

Hazel-nuts.   1½ tablespoons water.
8 ozs. brown sugar.   2 teaspoons vinegar.
2 ozs. butter or margarine.   2 tablespoons golden syrup.

Blanch nuts. Slightly dry and brown in oven.

Boil toffee ingredients together quickly twelve minutes. Test. If
sets, stir in as many nuts as toffee will take and hold together. Pour in
spoonfuls on buttered dish, or pour into buttered shallow tin.

SEAWEEDS
& MOSSES

CARRAGEEN OR IRISH MOSS 87
Carrageen Blanc-Mange 87; Carrageen Fruit Jelly 87

ROCK SAMPHIRE 88
Samphire Salad 89; Samphire Pickle 89

EDIBLE SEAWEEDS 90
Stewed Dulce 91; Sloke 91

CARRAGEEN OR IRISH MOSS

Carrageen is plentiful on our rocky northern coasts. An edible marine lichen containing sulphur and iodine. Wash well in several waters. Remove roots and dark stems. Half an oz. of the moss will set one and a half pints of liquid. In hot milk or water forms thick gelatinous paste which should be strained before using. Can be dried and kept airtight for winter use.

CARRAGEEN BLANC-MANGE

½ oz. prepared carrageen moss.   Flavouring.
1½ pints milk.   Sugar to taste.

Put moss and milk in saucepan. Bring to boil slowly. Stir well. Strain. Add flavouring and sugar. Turn into mould. Sets quickly.

CARRAGEEN FRUIT JELLY

The acid·of fruit, like vinegar, 'cuts' gelatine, therefore use only one pint of fresh fruit and juice or liquid to each ½ oz. of moss if firm set is required. Dissolve moss in fruit liquid. Strain and add fruit and sugar. Mould.

Carrageen jellies are always cloudy, though far more tasty than when made with commercial gelatine which has little food value.

¼ oz. of moss will thicken two pints of soup or gravy.

ROCK SAMPHIRE

Grows wild along sea coast. Is very aromatic and greatly aids digestion. Has been used for pickle for centuries.

It should be used young before it flowers. May and June are best months to look for it. The raw fleshy leaves have a salt spicy flavour.

Samphire

SAMPHIRE SALAD

Pickled Samphire.
Hard boiled eggs.
Sliced tomatoes.

Serve on crisp lettuce leaves with salad cream dressing.

SAMPHIRE PICKLE

Choose young green samphire. Steep in well-salted water twenty four
hours. Dry well on cloth. Arrange in jars.

Boil sufficient white wine vinegar with a little ginger, mace, and
allspice. Do not use too much.

Pour boiling water over samphire. Cover tightly when quite cold.
Ready for use in three weeks.

EDIBLE SEAWEEDS

Several of the seaweeds or sea vegetables found round our coast are edible and nourishing. Dulce and Sloke are the best. Both contain iodine and bromine.

Should be well washed in several lots of fresh water to remove gritty sand and small shells before using.

Edible Seaweeds

STEWED DULCE

Dulce has bright red broad fronds. Tastes somewhat like oysters. Put prepared weed in pan with lump of butter, pepper and salt, milk to cover, or mixture of milk and water if preferred. Simmer three to four hours till tender. Nearly all the liquid will have been absorbed. Cut into small pieces. Serve with fingers of brown bread toast or oatcakes.

SLOKE

Gather sloke, well wash, steep in fresh water with pinch of bicarbonate of soda. Drain. Put in pan with a little water in bottom. Cover and simmer several hours. Stir frequently. When soft add lump of butter, pepper and salt.

Serve with meat and potatoes as vegetable, or as separate dish with brown bread or oatcakes.

TRUFFLES
& MUSHROOMS

TRUFFLES

Sometimes called underground mushrooms. Are small edible tubers found in ground especially under beech and oak trees, always within a range limited to spread of branches.

In season November to March. At their best about Christmas time. English truffles are almost white, quite unlike the dark truffles of the Continent. They lose flavour quickly when taken from ground. Always store in box of earth if keeping only twenty-four hours.

To prepare them. Soak two hours in fresh water. Rinse and scrub well with brush. Reject any with musty smell. Fold in cloth till required.

Truffles

BUTTERED TRUFFLES

Thinly peel prepared truffles. Slice them. Put in pan with a little butter, chopped parsley and shallot, pepper and salt. Sauté ten minutes. Drain off fat. Add several tablespoons rich brown gravy, few drops lemon juice and pinch Cayenne pepper.

TRUFFLES A LA SERVIETTE

Select largest truffles. Prepare them. Put in pan with a little minced bacon, a bouquet garni of parsley, three spring onions, sprig of thyme, small bayleaf, two or three cloves. Cover with good white stock. Simmer gently one hour. Lift truffles out. Drain well. Serve dry on white napkin in very hot dish.

All small pieces or parings of truffle and stock in which cooked add delicious flavour to soups and savoury dishes.

FIELD MUSHROOMS

Field mushrooms can be eaten in two stages. As buttons, unopened, just as they rise from the spawn. Or expanding, when spore bearing ridges make a rosy lining to opened mushroom.

Wild mushrooms are very plump. If spores are black and flabby mushroom is overripe and should be avoided.

The poisonous kinds have white gills which do not join the stem. They have a thin frill-like ring round stem some distance from top.

Wild mushrooms can be used as cultivated ones for any recipe.

TO PICKLE WILD MUSHROOMS

Select tiny button mushrooms. Cut off bottom of stem. Wipe them clean with cloth. Lay them in cold white wine vinegar. Bring very slowly to boil. Drain well. When quite cold arrange them in glass jars. Cover with the scalded vinegar when it is cold. Cover and seal well.

* * *

SUBSTITUTES FOR FRESH LEMONS

Lemons are now unobtainable. For jams, puddings, etc.; any good lemon substitute purchased from a reliable chemist may be used.

For wines and beers a natural acid juice is required. Rhubarb juice, green-apple juice, or gooseberry juice are all useful substitutes.

* * *